AS IT USED TO BE: These two pages from Film Fun in the mid-1950s show that text stories were still published – and the Wild West was still popular.

This annual is for Dads only. All those Dads, that is, who are the fathers of boys and girls who read Christmas annuals. It's Dad's Own Annual, and it's all about the comics he read when he was the same age as his children – the comics of thirty-odd years ago.

For Dad it will be a trip back to his boyhood past, a different age, a different world.

Of course, lots of boys and girls will probably take a sneak look at it, too. And they'll probably laugh out loud at the things Dad used to read. But just imagine how their children will be laughing at their comics re-published in the Dad's Own Annual of the year 2023!

We're going to suppose that Dad was aged about ten in 1960. It doesn't matter if he was five or 15, he'll still have read and loved most of the comics we're reminiscing about. But because Dad was a reader of comics between about 1955 and 1965, that's the time we're going to talk most about.

SO SLIP INTO YOUR SLIPPERS, DAD, AND RELAX IN YOUR FAVOURITE ARMCHAIR. HERE WE GO!

£4.50

THE ADVERTISEMENTS

...and just look at the prices!

Although it was only about thirty years ago, it was a very different world. The Beatles were the pop music sensation of all time – each of their new releases was awaited with bated breath. There wasn't much television, and that was only in black and white. A variety show called Sunday Night at the Palladium was the TV event of the week. Liverpool were in the Second Division and £8,500 would buy a four bedroom, two bathroom detached house in a smart London suburb.

In those days many more boys read comics than they do today. And in a few more years' time, still more of them would be reading still more comics. By the time Dad was a teenager there were 50 weekly comics or magazines for boys and girls under 18 years old in the United Kingdom, and in one particular month their combined sales peaked at more than ten million copies a week.

Using as a measure comics and magazines which are strictly in the same age group today, the numbers would probably be only one-sixth of that figure of thirty years ago. So Dad was a great comics' reader, much more so than his son is today.

But viewed from behind the Editor's desk, Dad and his generation were a completely new and different kind of comic reader. For Dad's generation was the first to read comics which were composed entirely of picture strip stories. That made Dad himself something of a comic reading revolutionary.

There were 12 pence in a shilling and 20 shillings in a pound in these pre-decimilisation days. Air-fix kits were from 10 new pence; boys' football boots about £1.15p; Dinky Toys about 16p.

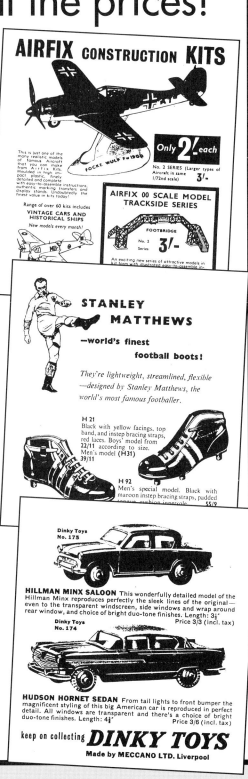

Restoration history and the Wild West were typical fare offered by the Sun comic (no relation to the daily newspaper). Note the high quality art-work, a feature of Fifties' comics.

EAGLE'S RIVALS...
with a real Fifties look

The "revolution" began in the 1940s. During the Second World War, and for many years after it, newsprint rationing severely curtailed the size of comics. Editors returning from military service in 1945 picked up their pens when they had left them in 1939. In those far-off days all comics, with the exception of some notable "funnies", had no picture strip stories. Instead, they were filled with text stories. So, the war over, the Editors went right on producing text stories - six, seven or eight a week in each issue, in serial form, and printed in the smallest type they knew – and for a few years everyone was happy.

But by the mid-Fifties the popularity of the cinema and the slow emergence of television were creating an appetite for more pictures and fewer words, an appetite that has grown and grown since that time. "Text" comics often contained every week more words than a long novel, and their weekly instalments – Wilson the Wonder Athlete; Rockfist Rogan, fighter pilot; Red Circle School, captained by the redoutable Dixie Dean, were some of them – were eagerly awaited by comic fans.

Dad wanted none of that. Dad wanted picture stories. The great text story writers faded away, and a new era, an era of the great boys' comic artists, was ushered in.

The writer wrote his script now not in simple text form, but describing it frame by frame, each frame incorporating dialogue and a paragraph or two of instructions to the artist on how to draw the frame.

ZETA IS ON P.7; WIDGEON HELICOPTER P.10; PRIZES P.15

EAGLE

EVERY WEDNESDAY

4½d

COMPANION TO GIRL, SWIFT AND ROBIN

8 NOVEMBER 1958 Vol. 9 No. 45

DAN DARE
PILOT OF THE FUTURE
in
THE PHANTOM FLEET

IT'S FAIR TORTURE STANDING HERE DOING NOTHING WITH COLONEL DAN SWALLOWED UP BY THAT LOT!

THE WIND'S SHIFTING THAT VAPOUR NORTHWARDS — AWAY FROM US. BY MY RECKONING, THE AREA WILL BE CLEAR WITHIN AN HOUR!

THE STORY SO FAR
The Cosmobes, refugees from I-Cos, settle in one of Earth's oceans. Their pursuers, the Pescods, possess a terrible weapon – The Crimson Death – a red cloud which melts metal. Spacemen wearing rubberized spacesuits – their only protection – stand-by in coastal areas. One Pescod craft 'hits the drink' near Lex O'Malley's ship, *Poseidon*, but he fails to destroy it. Another lands in Death Valley, California. Dan Dare, Sir Hubert Guest, Digby and volunteers set off to capture it, and 'Flamer' Spry, with Stripey, stows away aboard their troop-carrier. At Death Valley, Dan approaches the Pescod ship to test the rubberized spacesuits, and is completely enveloped by The Crimson Death!

OH, GOLLY! THERE GOES STRIPEY!

HEY, COME BACK!

BUT ONE FOUR-FOOTED VOLUNTEER FAILS TO UNDERSTAND SIR HUBERT'S ORDERS, AND SETS OFF ON A MISSION OF HIS OWN!

HE'S PICKED UP COLONEL DAN'S TRACKS!

STAND FAST, MEN!

COLONEL DARE HAS RISKED HIS LIFE TO TEST OUR NEW EQUIPMENT. WE *MUST* WAIT TO SEE THE RESULTS!

HE'S BARGING STRAIGHT INTO IT!

POOR LITTLE STRIPEY!

UNDISMAYED, STRIPEY TROTS ALONG DAN'S TRAIL . . .

. . . UNTIL HE, TOO, IS LOST IN THE DEADLY VAPOUR!

The combination that rocked the world of British comics

DAN DARE, here seen in his eighth great year, was still the front page fixture in Eagle, still priced here at the equivalent of less than two new pence. Hulton Press, publishers of Eagle, marketed its comics' "family" intelligently; thus this front cover proclaims Eagle's association with Girl, Swift and Robin.

TWO MEN - AND JUST A SINGLE THOUGHT

```
Page 1.
1.
The Match's Elton Welsby, wearing his
looking directly out at readers.

TITLE: UNITED!

STORY SO FAR BOX: BOTTOM CLUB UNITED
                  FIRST EVER SEASON I
                  MANAGER DANNY CASSI
                  WORLD TAKE NOTICE..

ELTON: WE DON'T OFTEN KICK OFF OUR GO
       BUT THEIR MARVELLOUS PERFORMAN
       EARNS THEM TOP BILLING...

2.
In Danny Cassidy's flat. With the TV
look back over it to Cassidy, bathed
screen. Despite the wordy build up fr
really paying attention, his mind pre

ELTON (JAGGED, TO TV): MANAGER DANNY
                       REFRESHING IDE
                       INJURIES LEAVE
                       SIMPLE, REALLY

CASSIDY: SOMETHING'S NOT RIGHT...FEEI
         THING...
```

Artist and writer worked together - but they may never have met!

The scripting system that came about with the advent of picture strip comics hasn't changed to this day. But it meant that two people, the artist and the writer, who perhaps never met each other throughout their working lives together, had to know exactly how the other thought.

The artist, for instance, had to know exactly what was in the writer's mind, far beyond the bland paragraph or two of instructions. And the writer had to know exactly how the artist was capable of interpreting the idea and the characters he was describing. He certainly couldn't drive to meet the artist in Edinburgh every week if he lived in Northampton, and more than likely the artist lived in Barcelona anyway. Oddly enough, the system worked, and still does.

The story began in the Editor's office, with the Editor talking over a script idea with a freelance picture-strip writer. The writer did his script, and, approved, it was sent to the artist or his agent. Back came the finished drawings – at this stage they were probably twice the size of a comic page. Approved, the drawings then went to the lettering artist, who created and lettered the balloons from the dialogue in the writer's script. Approved again, the pages finally went to press.

It went smoothly enough in theory, but hitches like having to send the art back to the artist for alterations were regular occurences. And it was, as you can imagine, immensely more time consuming and much more costly than producing a simple 6,000 word story instalment for a text comic. For a time it severely bruised the profits of comics' publishing – but for the publishers it was a case of get on the picture strip bandwagon or die. In fact, Dad and his "chums" (the Editor's favourite word for his readers!) quickly helped the profits to recover, because they liked picture strip comics and began to buy more and more of them.

When Dad became a comic reader he almost certainly began reading the boys' comic which, launched in 1951, revolutionised the traditional comics' publishing industry and made it never quite so traditional again.

That comic, of course, was "Eagle".

DAN'S FIRST NAME WAS LEX CHRISTIAN AND HIS EDITOR WAS A PARSON

magazine "Picture Post".

In the "dummy" of his boys' magazine "Eagle", Morris had the artwork of a new space age character drawn by Hampson. It says something for Morris and the direction in which he proposed to take the comic if he could find a publisher, that in this first dummy that character, who the world was to know as Dan Dare, had the working title of "Lex Christian".

*The first and hitherto only other photogravure colour comic was Mickey Mouse Weekly, launched in 1936 by Odhams Periodicals.

Everything about "Eagle" was amazing. It was the first post-war all colour photogravure comic*, and it was launched by a publisher who had no real experience of comic publishing. Its Editor was a parson who had never edited a comic before. In fact, the original concept was turned down by at least one major comic publisher, who must have spent the next 15 years gnawing his finger-nails to the quick.

One day in 1950 the Rev Marcus Morris set out from Lancashire with a young artist, Frank Hampson, in tow. They were bound for London, there to meet Sir Edward Hulton, chairman of Hulton's Press, a company then best-known for its famous illustrated news

For Dad's generation cricket rated above football. So, even in this late autumn Eagle Sports Page, when the soccer season was well under way, the cricket from Australia was given preferential coverage.

Sir Winston Churchill's biography in picture strip form and a biblical tale in similar style sat easily side by side in Eagle, edited by the Rev. Marcus Morris. Both stories were given excellence by their artist, Frank Bellamy, reckoned to be among the very best commercial artists of Eagle's day.

The HAPPY WARRIOR

The true life story of **SIR WINSTON CHURCHILL**

TOLD BY CLIFFORD MAKINS
DRAWN BY FRANK BELLAMY

June, 1944 — Second Front in Europe! On 6th June, a vast armada of ships carrying huge forces of British, Imperial and American troops crossed the Channel to assault the Normandy beaches, on the French coast. In spite of fierce resistance, successful landings are made everywhere. At noon on the same day, Prime Minister Churchill tells of these achievements to a crowded House of Commons...

AN IMMENSE ARMADA OF UPWARDS OF 4,000 SHIPS HAS CROSSED THE CHANNEL. MASSED AIRBORNE LANDINGS HAVE BEEN SUCCESSFULLY EFFECTED. THE FIRE OF SHORE BATTERIES HAS BEEN LARGELY QUELLED.

FOUR DAYS LATER...
MONTGOMERY REPORTS THAT HE'S WELL ENOUGH ESTABLISHED ON SHORE FOR US TO PAY HIM A VISIT.

SPLENDID! WE'LL GO RIGHT AWAY.

THE TIRELESS PREMIER WENT TO FRANCE.
WELCOME TO FRANCE, SIR!

THIS IS A GREAT MOMENT FOR US ALL! NOW, PLEASE MAY WE SEE THE SIGHTS!

GOOD OLD WINNIE!

WE HAVE PENETRATED ABOUT EIGHT MILES INLAND. THE TROOPS ARE IN FINE FETTLE.

Churchill returned to London, confident that the Allied campaign was well under way. Then, suddenly, the citizens of London were subjected to yet another ordeal...

THE FLYING BOMB!

CABINET MEETING.
LONDON IS SUFFERING BADLY FROM THESE 'DOODLE-BUGS'.

EXTENSIVE PLANS TO DESTROY THEM WILL SOON COME INTO FORCE.

BUT SHOULD WE CHANGE OUR STRATEGY IN FRANCE TO MEET THIS NEW THREAT?

FLYING BOMBS WERE LAUNCHED FROM SITES IN NORTHERN FRANCE...

CROSSED THE CHANNEL AT 400 MILES PER HOUR...

AND EXPLODED IN LONDON.

EARLY JULY. THE DECISIVE BATTLE OF CAEN...
ONCE CAEN IS CAPTURED, THE WAY INTO FRANCE IS WIDE OPEN. A GREAT BATTLE FOR THIS CITY IS NOW NEARING ITS CLIMAX.

NO, THAT IS JUST WHAT HITLER IS HOPING FOR. OUR STRATEGY REMAINS UNCHANGED. SOON WE WILL BREAK OUT OF NORMANDY AND CAPTURE THE FLYING BOMB SITES. MEANWHILE, LONDON CAN TAKE IT!

HITLER'S H.Q., MARGIVAL, FRANCE.
HERR FUEHRER, FIELD MARSHALS RUNSTEDT AND ROMMEL HAVE ARRIVED.

SEND THEM IN.

OUR ARMIES ARE BLEEDING TO DEATH IN NORMANDY. WE SHOULD WITHDRAW TO THE SEINE AND FIGHT THERE.

THE ALLIED AIR FORCES OVERWHELM US NIGHT AND DAY. IT IS TERRIFYING!

NO-NO! THERE MUST BE NO RETREAT. THE ARMY MUST FIGHT AND DIE WHERE IT STANDS. OUR FLYING BOMBS WILL SOON BRING BRITAIN TO HER KNEES!

TO BE CONTINUED.

EAGLE WAS PERCEIVED AS HAVING 'CLASS'

– and in the Fifties it was class that counted...

Like many comics, the Comet offered cash for readers' jokes. Comet, like its companion publication the Sun Comic, was in a smaller format than traditional comics – a format that never caught on.

Edward Hulton didn't particularly want to publish comics. He didn't know anything about them. But he wanted to publish something. Like many magazine publishers of his day he was also a printer and like many publisher–printers he filled his expensive machines simply by publishing periodicals to suit them.

It's a formula that would work well enough in a Utopian world. But when the magazines the publisher is printing are not being bought, he has to keep on publishing at a loss just to keep his printing presses busy. Then, because the printing presses are no longer competitive, the printer starts charging his customer – who is, of course, himself as publisher – more than the publisher can afford, thus putting the magazines in the red. Generally speaking, publishers today, aware of this forked hazard, are no longer also printers.

But in Hulton's day they were, and in his rotogravure presses Hulton had the most expensive form of colour printing in existence – the sort of machines that can give their owner sleepless nights when they're standing idle. He had to print, even if it also meant he had to publish.

There was another problem. Rotogravure presses at that time were not generally economical at print runs under 300,000 copies, because of the high cost of preparing the copper cylinders that carry the impression of the pages. Other printing processes were used for below 300,000 copy runs, but that wasn't Hulton's business.

A glance at the market would have shown Hulton that while there were comics like Beano and Dandy that were selling well in excess of 300,000 a week, they were well-established and had remarkably low cover prices. In the post-war austerity years many foodstuffs were still on ration; Britons were used to low prices and poor quality. A photogravure all-colour comic would be a bold venture, and if there were to be such a thing its cover price would have to reflect its high cost of production. What this added up to was that Hulton would have to sell an awful lot of "Eagles", and at a price well above the market average.

Added to that he was pitching in against the two giants of comic publishing that dominated the British scene. The Amalgamated Press in London, with its roots back in the nineteenth century, and D.C. Thomson in Dundee, another long-established company, had sewn up the comics' marker. A clergyman as Editor, an unified senior artist ... it hardly seemed possible.

It was just the sort of challenge Hulton rose to. If publishing is about "gut feel", Hulton was one of those men who instinctively knew what would work. In the end, he printed something short of a million of the first issue of Eagle, and it was a sell-out. If you have one in your attic, Dad, it's probably worth a couple of hundred pounds.

You could immediately identify its unique selling points – U.S.Ps in the buzz-terminology of the day. In those austerity years its gleaming photogravure colour pages were a shining beacon in a world of comics built on shabby letterpress printed on newsprint paper – black and white pages that succeeded in looking uniformly grey. It had Dan Dare, and Hampson was an excellent artist – although by no means as brilliant as has been suggested – when he could be persuaded to keep up with an exacting weekly schedule. The story, with its Digby and the Mekon, might seem old hat today, but in the Fifties it was new and sparkling, and Dan Dare was certainly the prototype of many a hero–and–villain space story that has thrilled subsequent generations.

It had, too, a remarkable centre spread in the "exploded" drawings of L. Ashwell Wood, who took the Flying Scotsman railway engine, or a Churchill tank, and pulled off the layers to show the works. This was to be, with Dan Dare, Eagle's longest running series, and one that would have been immeasurably improved if, besides just showing the works, it showed how the thing worked.

It also had Pc 49, a black and white strip b on a popular radio serial, and The Story of Pa (St. Paul, that is), neither of which would have been regarded by rival publishers as circulatio magic, even in the Fifties.

Undoubtedly colour and cover price set Eagle a class apart, and undoubtedly class had a lot do with it. For some reason that probably nee psychologist's viewpoint, the very large numb of educational institutions which in the 1950s banned all comics from their premises, happily excluded this newcomer from that proscription Yet Eagle was a comic, and didn't claim to be anything else. Either, then, they were fooled by the look of the thing, or by the high cover price by the Rev. Marcus Morris's credentials, which were certainly different from those of the Editor Beano or Lion.

If Dad had come to Eagle in the mid-1950s, fo or five years after its launch, he would have bee reading what was still a best-seller and still probably the most profitable comic in the U.K. I he came to it ten years later, he would have found that the rot had well and truly set in.

After fifteen years Eagle was in the doldrums The Rev. Marcus Morris was now Managing Director of National Magazines and Hampson had finally succumbed to what was for him the wearisome struggle of maintaining a weekly schedule: four different artists were now drawing Dan Dare and the great space age hero of yesteryear was looking distinctly plump and old-fashioned.

Stripped of their brilliant colour, these two Eagle stories neither read or look any better than similar stories in rival comics. But colour transformed them, and Eagle was ahead of all its opposition as a colour comic

THE BIG BLOW-UPS

THE 1½ LITRE PORSCHE SPYDER SPORTS/RACING CAR

The late Dr Ferdinand Porsche was one of the world's most eminent designer/engineers in the motor-car industry. Famed for his theories in regard to rear-engined vehicles, he was mainly responsible for the remarkable Auto Union Grand Prix cars of revolutionary design and appearance which raced with such outstanding success in the years immediately prior to World War II.

Today his son, Dr Ferry Porsche, continues to develop his father's ideas, incorporating many of his own. The *Porsche Spyder* is one of the modern products of this famous Stuttgart firm, and these tiny silver projectiles are universally regarded as being among the most highly successful 1½ litre Sports Racing cars in existence. During the 1957 racing season, Porsche cars won over 700 International successes!

BRITAIN'S NEW SUPERSONIC JET FIGHTER
(THE ENGLISH ELECTRIC P.1B)

In this special drawing of the latest supersonic jet fighter, only those parts and details are shown that are permitted by security regulations.

The English Electric P.1B all-weather day and night fighter has been ordered for quantity production for the R.A.F., and is destined to follow present-day fighters into squadron service. It may be the last of the piloted fighters to go into production because of the advance in ground-to-air guided missiles as interceptors. The P.1B is powered by two Rolls-Royce Avon jet engines of a new type, one above the other in the fuselage. Its extensive armament includes air-to-air guided missiles. Performance figures are secret.

KEY TO THE POWER INSTALLATION: (1) Air intakes to engines all round centre cone of nose. (2) Air duct to upper and lower engines. (3) Lower Rolls-Royce Avon jet engine with afterburners. (4) Engine starter. (5) Sixteen stage air compressor. (6) Annular combustion chamber. (7) Three stage turbine. (8) Upper Rolls-Royce Avon jet engine with afterburners. (9) Upper engine jet pipe to afterburner. (10) Upper engine afterburner. Here the expanding exhaust gases from the engine are again ignited, giving extra thrust. (11) Lower engine jet pipe to afterburner. (12) Lower engine afterburner. (13) Lower jet exhaust pipe. (14) Upper jet exhaust pipe.

KEY TO OTHER PARTS: (15) Connection for drag parachute used for retarding aircraft when landing. (16) Fin and rudder. (17) Swept back tailplane. (18) Tail bumper. (19) Tailplane operating jack. Both tailplanes are moved as elevators. (20) Ventral (under the belly) fuel tank. (21) Port air brake flap (extended). (22) Split flap on trailing edge of swept back wing. (23) Aileron. (24) Main undercarriage wheel retracted. (25) 'Hockey-stick' shaped main wing spar. (26) Cockpit floor over air duct. (27) Nose wheel retracted into space under centre cone. (28) Radar in centre cone. (29) Pilot air pressure booms. (30) De Havilland Firestreak infra-red, air-to-air guided missiles being fired.

ENGLISH ELECTRIC P.1B
Two Rolls-Royce Avon engines.
Span: 34ft. 10ins.
Length: 48ft. 2ins.

DESIGNED TO THRILL

In the 42nd Targa Florio - held in May, 1958, over 600 miles of tortuous Sicilian mountain roads - a *Porsche Spyder* driven by the brilliant Frenchman Jean Behra, and co-driver Scarlatti, put up an amazing performance by beating cars of far greater power to achieve second place! One of the great classics of racing history, the Targa Florio was first held in 1906 and, with only minor breaks necessitated by war, has been held annually in one form or another every year since that date. An added hazard for drivers in the early days of the race were the 'trigger happy' local bandits, who often took 'pot-shots' at the passing cars!

KEY TO NUMBERED PARTS: (1) Finned drum of the Teves hydraulic brakes. (2) Telescopic double-acting shock-absorber. (3) Anti-roll bar. (4) Upper laminated torsion bar. (5) Track rod. (6) ZF-Gemmer worm and ball steering box. (7) Universally jointed steering-column. (8) Driving mirror. (9) Fuel tank. (10) Perspex wrap-round windscreen. (11) Sprung steering-wheel. (12) Duplicate fuel pumps. (13) Clutch pedal. (14) Foot-brake pedal. (15) Throttle pedal. (16) Hand brake. (17) Tubular chassis frame. (18) Battery. (19) Alloy body-shell. (20) Bulkhead. (21) Camshaft and valve gear covers of the 4 cylinder air-cooled engine. Capacity, 1,498 c.c. Power output, 130 b.h.p. at 7,000 r.p.m. (22) Lower camshaft and valve gear covers are fitted with cooling fins. (23) Disc wheels with 5-stud fixing. (24) Racing tyres. (25) Rear swing axle. (26) Telescopic double-acting shock-absorber. (27) Bosch distributor (one each side). (28) Downdraft Weber carburettor (two ~ one each side). (29) Casing of high-speed, ducted cooling fan. (30) Oil tank. (31) Crankcase breather. (32) Bosch twin ignition coils. (33) Starter motor. (34) Half-shaft universals. (35) Differential/gearbox unit, enclosing Porsche syncromesh on all four gears. (36) Stabilizing fins. (37) Engine ventilation grille.

EAGLE was the first boys' comic to use artist - draughtsmen, and L. Ashwell Wood's "cutaways", as they were called, became the hallmark of the publication's centre spread. Other artists were occasionally used, as in the case of the Porsche drawn here by J. Fisher.

"Cutaways" looked good and perhaps gave the reader a feeling of technical superiority over other comics' readers.

But their "keys", always written by the technical artist himself and apparently never edited, must have been mumbo-jumbo to a nine-year-old reader of Dad's generation, puzzling over the unexplained meaning of "half shaft universals" and "crankcase breather".

Like Eagle, Film Fun ran for 20 years, but its day was nearly over when Dad was a boy. Film Fun persisted to the end with captions which added nothing to the story after you had read the "speech balloons".

Towards the end of its long career, Eagle was taken over by Odhams Periodicals, which had bought the Hulton Press, and its new stable companions were an odd assortment of mishmash called Pow! Wham! and Smash. On top of that, a rapid succession of Editors with a range of different ideas were eroding the comic's initial identity.

Truth to tell, from the day it was launched, Eagle's circulation never went up – only down. The sales figure of its first issue was, however, so high, that it could continue to fall every week and still be there nearly 20 years later. When in 1970 it was ignominiously merged into the letterpress comic, Lion, it was unrecognisable from its former self.

Another long-running weekly, Radio Fun tried to combine radio characters like Jimmy Edwards, star of "Whacko!" with 'own-brand' stories, producing a curious mixture of history and the Wild West. The radio characters became fewer, the historical stories more numerous, as this famous comic plunged to its death.

RADIO FUN - BUT IT WASN'T ALWAYS ON THE WIRELESS!

MEANWHILE, DAD'S YOUNGER BROTHER ALSO HAD HIS OWN COMIC...

Jack and Jill 4d

EVERY MONDAY

No. 39
November 20, 1954

Jack and Jill of Buttercup Farm

The twins and Patch run through the rain
And meet a stray horse in the lane.

"We'll find its master, if we can,"
Says Jack: "Oh, look—a caravan!"

"Nursery" titles boomed in the Fifties. Unencumbered by television characters, they achieved several hundreds of thousands of sales per publication weekly, at the same cover price as a boys' comic but with half the number of pages.

Jack and Jill, launched in 1954, was a particular favourite. Big pictures, lots of colour and as few words as possible made them popular as a parent-purchase. "Jolly Jingles" was on the back cover of Jack and Jill Weekly. Strangely, "nursery" titles were a target in the next decade of consumer pressure groups. The Jack and Jill story "Dr David and Nurse Susan" was the subject of a number of complaints about stereotyping.

Jolly Jingles

"Hooray!" the Jolly Miller sings:
   "Now that our work is done,
Let's have some sport. To make a start
   A sack race will be fun."

"Bring me a hat!" says Old King Cole,
   "My crown is much too tight."
They bring a hat which is too big—
   He vanishes from sight.

"Good gracious me, what goes on here?"
   Asks dear old Mother Hubbard.
"There's Fido skating round the floor
   And toys are in my cupboard."

Tommy Tucker spends his playtime
   Sitting at his window high,
Looking down upon the rail

When Harold Hare declared that he would like a girl relative to make his morning cup of tea, "because that's what girls are for," the publishers received an official complaint from the Equal Opportunities Commission. Another group of characters who sent their tiresome old granny to the moon on a rocket on Guy Fawkes' Night were also the subject of an official complaint – aired on television – for misusing fireworks.

Despite their detractors, "nursery" comics remained a strong part of the comics' market until they were swept away by the overwhelming pull of television character – based comics in the 1980s.

Top of the pops among the "off-beat" stories that were beloved of Fifties' and Sixties' comics was Lion's "The Steel Claw". The claw belonged to Louis Grandell, who could become invisible all except for his artificial hand. Grandell was at first a "baddie" who used his chilling power for evil. But a later editorial decision to turn him into a "goodie" produced much better story-lines.

While Dad was avidly devouring his average 2.4 comics a week, a very large and extraordinarily withdrawn press tycoon named Cecil Harmsworth King was Chairman of the Daily Mirror. King was a relative of the late Lord Northcliffe, who began his journalistic career with the U.K's biggest comics' publisher, the Amalgamated Press; in the classic contemporary cliche, ink was therefore in his blood. So, while Dad studied the weekly Eagle, King decided to buy three magazine publishing houses: Odhams Press (which had become the owners of Eagle), George Newnes, and the Amalgamated Press.

IT'S NOT WORKING! THE CHARGE WASN'T POWERFUL ENOUGH! I'M STILL VISIBLE!

...ATH-TAKING STORY NEXT WEEK!

13

Between them, these three houses published more than 80 per cent of all the magazines read in the U.K. Odhams published some comics besides Eagle, but the Amalgamated Press had the lion's share – around 45 per cent of the U.K. market.

Later on, King was to roll up his three acquisitions into one company, called IPC Magazines Ltd., but that is outside the scope of our story. For the moment "planned competition" was the buzz pharse. The Amalgamated Press changed its name to Fleetway Publications, and three or four of its comics' editorial staff were despatched to Odhams to see what could be done with the comics that company had inherited in its earlier take-over of Hulton's.

Besides Eagle, these included Swift, Girl, and Robin, and all were on the slippery slope to oblivion. The new strategy evolved was that Odhams should develop comics from this stable in opposition to the giant Fleetway – for King had decreed that the competitive edge between the three companies would be retained, although obviously controlled centrally. So, in quick succession the ailing quartet led by Eagle were joined by Smash, Pow, and Wham, three comics that looked like nothing much else on the British market and which Dad and his chums quickly rejected.

Now there is nothing more likely to precipitate the descent of a loser than to have it surrounded by other losers. Thus it was with "Eagle". The new Odhams comics' executives badly wanted to make something of the Odhams comics' stable, if only to show their comrades in Fleetway House that they were the better men. But the Odhams management, with the top-selling women's weekly magazine "Woman" at the head of their flagpole, had more urgent priorities for their cash; they didn't care about comics.

And so, if Dad was getting any enjoyment out of Smash Wham and Pow and the dying Eagle he wasn't going to get it for very long. They were about to fall over each other into the comics' graveyard. The rump of Odhams comics was merged into the new Fleetway company in 1970 and one of the management's first acts was to administer the *coup de grace* to the terminally ill Eagle. Ironically it was selling 60,000 copies a week – enough to make any comic in the 1990s highly successful.

Interestingly, there is a school of latter-day thought that the launch and success of Eagle, widely hailed as the biggest fillip to the comics' industry in the second half of the twentieth century, was in fact a disaster for it. The reasoning runs like this:

In the 1950s comics faced their first onslaught from the new competitive media – television. There were then, as now, children's programmes which some children watched, and adult programmes which many children watched. There were new characters, "in" phrases, and moving pictures – you didn't have to make the effort to read. The new sub-literate culture was just about breaking its birth-water when Dad was a boy. But for the time being comics and television did co-exist.

THE FAMILY THAT THRILLED 'JACK AND JILL' READERS

'Nursery' comics ran their favourite stories year in and year out. The editorial thinking was that little children disliked change, and so if a story was accepted and liked, it should be left to run.
One of Jack and Jill's longest running stories was 'The Old Woman who lived in a shoe', in which the old woman's many children appeared each week in some new situation.
One of them was always reading, one was always drawing, one was always eating, and so on. The object of the exercise for Dad's younger brother or sister was to spot these regulars.

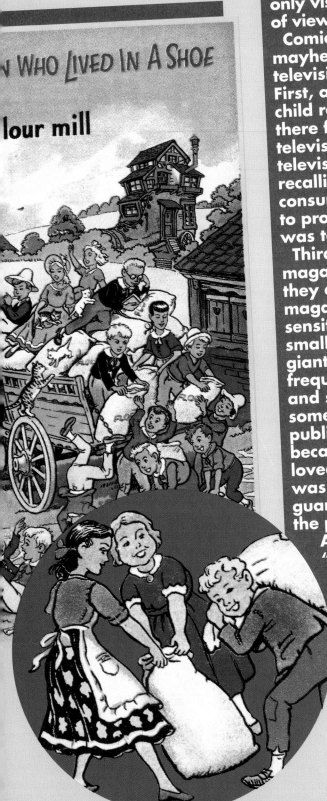

WHO LIVED IN A SHOE

lour mill

In the Fifties and Sixties it was clear that television was going to get rough. Violence, murder, brutality slowly seeped through the adult programmes that some children watched, and were only visibly toned down after a chain of viewer reactions in the 1980s.

Comics looked on helplessly at this mayhem. They were unable to copy television for a number of reasons. First, a "horror" frame frozen for a child reader on a comics' page was there for all to see, unlike the fleeting television image that critics of television sometimes had difficulty recalling. Second, it was easier for the consumer pressure groups that began to proliferate to take on comics than it was to take on television.

Third, comics were published by magazine companies, which, because they also published popular Women's magazines and were "image sensitive", were more vulnerable to small-time criticism than television giants. Fourth, these pressure groups, frequently composed of ill-advised and superficial thinkers and sometimes composed of blatant publicity-seekers, recognised that because everyone once read and loved comics, any criticism of them was automatically hot news guaranteed to get someone's name in the papers.

And fifth, so the cynics hold, was "Eagle". For "Eagle" had partly blocked the way that comics should go if they were in any way to challenge television at its own game.

Eagle had actually set the clock back. Its strengths were Dan Dare and lots of glossy colour, but its indelible puritanism was against the media trend. Whether you agreed or disagreed with that trend was irrelevant. The portrayal of greater realism, which inevitably meant some violence, was becoming statutory in television programmes that were watched by children and, unable to make up their minds whether to go the Eagle way or the television way, comics temporarily fell apart. By the time they recovered they had already lost the battle with TV that they could probably never have won.

EDUCATION WITH A KICK IN IT

As Dad grew into his teens, the first serious answer to the gravure colour onslaught on the children's market from Eagle and its later stable companions Swift, Robin and Girl was launched by the new Fleetway company, which had been born out of the old Amalgamated Press.

It was called Look and Learn. Like Eagle it was something entirely new. It was destined to last 21 years – a year longer than Eagle, and although it might not have sold quite so many copies every week, it was financially far more successful than the Hulton Press comic.

Look and Learn was inspired by the weekly part-work Knowledge, rather than by Eagle. Knowledge, originated by an Italian company, was launched on to the British market in the late Fifties. As with all part-

works it was programmed to last for a specified period and published as a "collectable" – a compendium of rather expensive information which you filed weekly in your binder. In the case of Knowledge the planned publishing period was for two years, and the cover price, two shillings, (10p) was breathtakingly high.

Knowledge was definitely for the "swots" as Dad would have called them, but it was also a great success. It was published in a number of countries, and subsequently re-published for its full two-year span three

THE SUB-LIEUTENANT LAID THE CHARGES . . . BUT IT WAS HURRICANE WHO EXPLODED!

Sales of picture strip comics remained unaffected by the popularity of educational weeklies. And the Second World War continued to be the favourite story subject. The heroics of Captain Hurricane thrilled Dad's generation in Tiger. Later, this square-jawed Rambo of the British Marines was retired, and the long-running weekly comic became an all-sports publication.

The approach was ever-so-slightly brash – the message to readers was that you could get a kick out of education. Sample headlines from a series about unsubstantiated historical stories which attempted to weigh the evidence for what really happened: "Nero Never Played a Note that Night", and "Some Black Marks for the Black Prince".

The purists were probably shocked, but the readers were delighted. Look and Learn sold nearly 400,000 copies of its first issue. A year later it was still selling 350,000 a week, a much more shallow first year decline in sales than was usually experienced by a traditional comic.

Among its avowed admirers was the late A.J.P. Taylor, a celebrated modern history Oxford don, and the Prince of Wales, who had his weekly copy delivered to Buckingham Palace throughout his schoolboy years. When some winners of a Look and Learn contest were brought to London for their prize-giving, the Prince happily agreed to present the awards, which was unprecedented royal recognition for a children's magazine.

more times in the U.K. It was the very first of the post Second World War popular part-works, a form of specialised publishing still carried on today, and which, incidentally, began before Dad was born, in the 1930s.

Daringly, Fleetway decided with their Look and Learn that there was room for another educational weekly – but as an "open-ended" magazine printed like Eagle in photogravure, and priced at one shilling (5p), then four times the price of a comic.

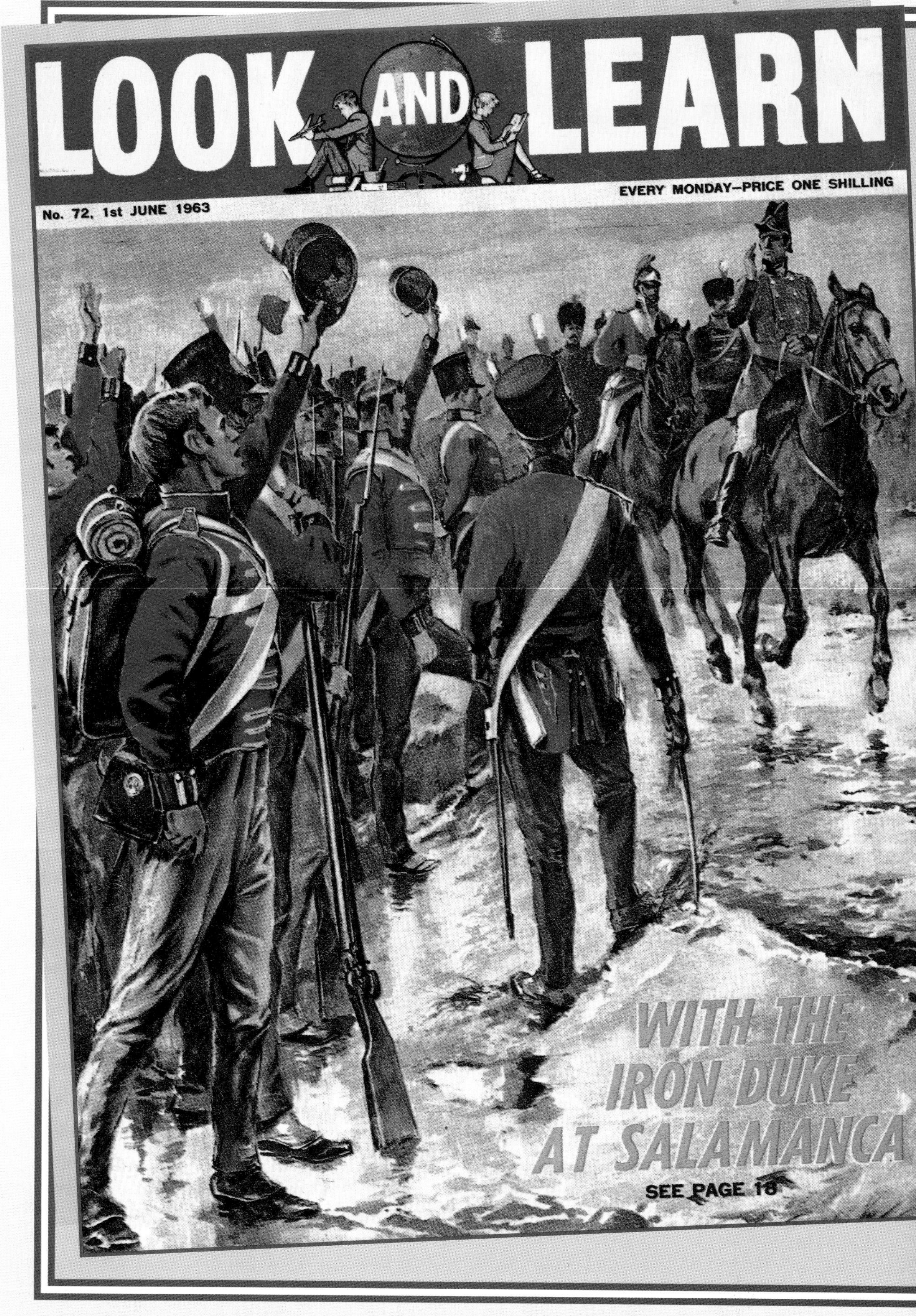

LOOK AND LEARN

EVERY MONDAY—PRICE ONE SHILLING

No. 72, 1st JUNE 1963

WITH THE IRON DUKE AT SALAMANCA

SEE PAGE 18

FACING UP TO BEAUTY

The Story of Cosmetics

Egyptian women had discovered the use of beauty aids, or "cosmetics," as long ago as 5000 B.C. To make their eyes lovelier and larger, they painted eyebrows and lashes with a black dye called kohl and tinted the skin around them green, using small wooden or ivory sticks.

A white skin was considered beautiful by Greek women, who used chalk or poisonous white lead on their faces. For contrast they dyed their lashes with kohl and used a rouge called *fucus* for cheeks and lips. Skin rashes were disguised with barley flour and butter, teeth whitened with pumice stone.

Cold cream, to keep the skin supple, was used in Europe as early as the first century A.D. Roman women applied it liberally, and they also perfumed their skin with rose and almond flower petals soaked in olive oil. They even discovered a preparation for bleaching their hair.

When knights returned from the Crusades in the East they brought back many of the beauty secrets used by the Oriental women there—kohl for the eyes, red henna for the fingernails, and creams far superior to English cosmetics.

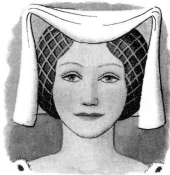

It was fashionable to shape the eyebrows in the Middle Ages to emphasize the eyes. The poison belladonna was used as an eyewash to make women's eyes brighter, and dangerous substances like white lead were used to lighten the skin.

Elizabethan women kept their cosmetics in perfumed boxes called "sweet coffers." Many of the ointments they used were too harsh, but for extra beauty they bathed in milk and washed their faces in wine.

Women were discouraged from using cosmetics during the rule of Oliver Cromwell, but they came back into fashion after the Restoration. Both court ladies and men painted their faces and used black patches to cover blemishes. They powdered their hair white.

Later little books of papers coated with fine rice-powder, called *papier poudre*, were used for shiny faces. But stern Victorian parents disapproved of cosmetics and kept a wary eye on daughters who tried to powder their faces in this way before a ball. "Painted" women were very much frowned upon.

Today the art of make-up is a science in itself. The skin of the face is fed and improved by ingredients in creams, lipsticks, powder, eye-shadow, mascara and face-pack. But many of the old ingredients remain—toothpaste, for instance, contains both chalk and pumice.

22

Look and Learn was the first post - Second World War educational magazine for children and was an outstanding success. Aimed at nine to fifteen year olds, it was also widely read by parents. An Editor remarked, "We used to get lots of letters saying, 'I am writing on behalf of my son Tommy', when clearly from what followed the writer was writing on behalf of themselves". *Look and Learn's* unisex appeal is illustrated in these two pages.

The big colour picture and the short sentence were Look and Learn hallmarks. The story of Scott of the Antarctic appeared under "Stories of Courage"; how the atom was split was flagged "Secrets of Life". The exploded colour centre spread diagram pioneered by Eagle was now developed into a random lay-out colour spread telling the story of York Minster or the Tower of London. The magazine – for this truly was a magazine as distinct from a comic – harvested the very best artists from a global crop. They included Reggirio Giovannini and Fortunino Matania in Italy, and in England Ron Embleton, Don Lawrence, Neville Dear – there were at least a dozen U. K. fine artists on the regular contributors' list.

Dad may have learned a great deal from Look and Learn, but he was probably grown up and starting out to work when, fired by their success, the publishers successfully launched the publication's educational "junior", called Treasure. Then came Tell Me Why, World of Wonder, Now I Know – the young Briton's appetite for education seemed insatiable.

R HAD A SCORE TO SETTLE . . . WITH CAPTAIN BRETT BLADE !

BLADE of the FRONTIER

At Fort Kuram, on the North-West Frontier of India, the famous officer, Captain Brett Blade, was awaiting the arrival of his friend Captain Frost, who was escorting a villainous gun-runner called Sam Jerker . . .

SUN-SCORCHED AND A WILD-EYED SWEAT-STAINED THE MAN CAST A GLANCE OVER HIS SHOULDER, AS IF ON HIS

O MERCIFUL HEAVEN! DON'T LET THOSE DEMONS GET ME! I COULDN'T STAND IT! I COULDN'T STAND IT!

THE HUSKY SERGEANT'S EYES WIDENED AT THE MENTION OF KRISNA BADAL... HE WAS A WAR-CRAZY FIEND, WHOSE CRUEL TREATMENT OF HIS CAPTIVES MADE HIM HATED BY EVEN HIS FELLOW TRIBESMEN.

KRISNA BADAL! BY GLORY! IS THAT DEMON CUTTING UP ROUGH AGAIN? I THOUGHT HE'D BE LYING LOW AFTER CAPTAIN BLADE AND CAPTAIN FROST BROUGHT HIS BROTHER TO JUSTICE!

Unperturbed by the rush to buy educational magazines, picture picture strip comics like Hurricane went on as usual. "Blade of the Frontier" was one of Hurricane's most popular stories. Blade was Captain Brett Blade, and the Frontier was in North West India.

Billy Bunter, the Fat Owl of the Remove at Greyfriars School, was the 1920s creation of Charles Hamilton, who wrote the long Greyfriars text stories under the name of Frank Richards in the Magnet, published by the Amalgamated Press before the Second World War. The Magnet ceased publication in 1940, a victim of newsprint rationing, but after the war Fleetway brought back Bunter in picture strip form, first in Knockout in the mid-Fifties. During this period Fleetway were selling some of their picture strip stories to Spaarnestad, then Holland's biggest comics' publisher. One day in the late Fifties, Spaarnestad hastily ordered a batch of stories, and a Bunter story was sent in error. It was too late to get the original order processed, and with nothing else to fill the blank spaces in his comic, which was due at press, the Dutch editor decided he would have to use the Bunter story, calling its hero Billy Turf.

"It was about a fat boy at an English public boarding school, a situation which no Dutch child could possibly understand", the editor said. "I closed my eyes and prayed that none of my readers would notice the new story, which I would drop as soon as the order was correctly sent". The Dutch editor was wrong. Billy Turf became a hero of Dutch comics' readers – and was popular in Holland for 25 years.

THIS WONDERFUL WORLD

SWIFT: A COMIC WELL BELOW THE DIZZY HEIGHTS OF EAGLE

Four years after launching Eagle, Hulton Press started its first companion publication, Swift. The newcomer had no Dan Dare and no 'exploded' technical drawings – indeed, nothing in it was good enough to catch the reader's eye for long.

These Swift features show how the drawings were much below Eagle's standards and how the story lines (a reindeer receiving a smile as it wonders if it might have some coffee?) were at least improbable.

Swift never achieved Eagle's fame, although it had the benefit of full-colour photogravure printing. It was the least successful of the Hulton quartet of Eagle, Swift, Girl and Robin.

IN OTHER LANDS No 8

FINLAND
The reindeer looks inside the cosy tent at the boy sipping his coffee and wonders if he might have some too. Mother smiles at the reindeer as she rocks her baby to sleep.

That evening. Ah! There's Rex just sliding into his cannon. The Rolling Stones must have got hold of a new net for him somehow!

Rex! You! B-b-but..?

Yes, it's me all right. And I must say those Rolling Stones are an amazing family!

SEE INSIDE! FUN! EXCITEMENT! THRILLS!

Swift

COMPANION TO EAGLE, GIRL & ROBIN

VOL 1 No 36 **4D** EVERY
20 NOVEMBER 1954 TUESDAY

PUBLISHED WEEKLY BY HULTON PRESS LTD

TARNA *Jungle Boy*

Why do you think they have made us prisoners, Toto? We have done nothing to them!

Tarna and his chimpanzee friend, Toto, find a treasure map leading to Golden Mountain. They reach a fishing village, the fifth place on the map, in their sand-yacht. The natives of the village capture them and tie them up

Hush! My brothers did wrong to treat you like this. I will release you!

All the fishermen think there are evil spirits living on Lonely Island, because of strange noises. Why are you going there?

We're following a map. It says we'll find a reward on Golden Mountain.

It is very dangerous to go there, but as you are determined, I will help you! Follow me!

My fishing boat is on the shore.

I will go with you, for if I stay here, I shall surely be killed for letting you escape.

I think it has been discovered already!

Start rowing, quickly!

Children's Newspaper

ren's Newspaper, Week Ending August 10, 1957

FOUNDED BY ARTHUR MEE

No. 2003, August 10, 1957

ry Wednesday—Threepence

BERMONDSEY BOY WHO BECAME A STAR

Max Bygraves talks to the C N

NG in his dressing-room—the star dressing-room A of
ne London Palladium, Max Bygraves put on his glasses
he talked to a C N correspondent.
, always wear these off-stage; I just have to, couldn't see
thing otherwise," he chuckled.

It was a typical Max Bygraves
remark. Although he is probably
the highest paid entertainer in this
country today, famous on the
stage, in T V, records, and radio,
not forgetting films, he is as cheer-
ful, quiet, and modest a man as
you could meet.

He is still prepared to talk
about those times only nine years
ago when all the money he had
in the world was 5s. 9d.—he remembers the exact sum—and he
had two small babies

Chaplin in the street to the amusement of a bunch of kids.

"'That boy of yours ought to
be on the stage,' she said to my
mother. 'On the stage'—that
phrase seemed to stick in my mind.
Ever after that I was hanging
around anywhere where there was
music and dancing and entertainment. I sang solo in the school
choir and at church. I sang at
kids' concerts. And as I got older
I went in for all the children's
talent competitions I could find."

THE NEWS FOR KIDS

One non-comic publication with a quasi-educational basis that was resisitant to all modernisation had been a publishing legend in its heydey. For decades The Children's Newspaper, published by the Amalgamated Press, had survived every sort of market shift, and while Dad was avidly reading his picture-strip comics, the C.N., as it was called, was still up there alongside them on the bookstall shelves.

A weekly publication, The Children's Newspaper had distinguished itself under its first editor Arthur Mee, reaching its popularity peak before Dad was born, in the 1930s. Mee came down to Fleet Street from Nottingham while still in his teens and plunged into his chosen journalistic career as popular educator.

Mee showed remarkable courage and foresight with his black and white tabloid newspaper. "Who will stop the greedy ambitions of this tyrant Adolf Hitler?" he thundered on page one in the early Thirties, at a time when world leaders were genuflecting to the German dictator. Then, in an adjacent story on the same page, he would report in glowing terms on Lord Baden Powell's visit to the latest Scout jamboree.

But by the time Dad arrived on the scene Mee was dead and his famous newspaper was looking sick and sorry. Even the hustle-bustle salesmen who sold bulk copies to school headmasters at a discount so that the Head could persuade his pupils to buy it and make himself a bit of cash on the side were finding no takers. Mee's editorial successors – all but one of the Editors who succeeded him had been trained on The Children's Newspaper by Mee himself – were unable to shake off the master's now hopelessly dated touch.

And so "C.N.", much loved in its time and now a victim of Sixties fashion, died at the end of the decade, mourned only by its 30,000 last readers.

COMIC CUTS:
Some golden oldies went on and on

Launched in 1890, Comic Cuts was still staggering on when Dad was at school. This is what it looked like in the Fifties. In the 19th Century line blocks were called 'cuts' – hence the comic's name.

If Dad was at school in the late 1950s, or the early 1960s, he will undoubtedly remember the Beano, Dandy and Topper. They were the front runners in the U.K. funny comics' market, and three of the jewels in the impressive crown of D.C. Thomson, the private publishing house in Dundee.

That these three comics made an indelible impression on their readers is perhaps no better illustrated than by the fact that five or six years ago the men responsible for drawing up the international airways' rules over the North Sea were asked to give names to new high reporting points between London and Oslo and London and Amsterdam. The stipulation, for technical reasons, was that each name had to be exactly five letters.

Hence, today airline captains over the North Sea report from Beano, Dandy, Eagle and Toppa – the last being Topper converted into five letters.

Faced with low price "humour" comics with good quality editorial from the secretive but highly competitive D.C. Thomson machine, Fleetway closed Chips, Comic Cuts, Film Fun, Knockout, Radio Fun and several others, and made a conscious decision to steer clear of that market area.

VALIANT
6d

FAMOUS FIGHTERS

**EVERY MONDAY
24th NOVEMBER, 1962**

THE BATTLE OF BRITAIN PILOTS

THE HAWKER 'HURRICANE' WAS BRITAIN'S CHIEF DEFENCE AGAINST THE GERMAN AIRFLEETS IN THE AUTUMN OF 1940. THIS 8-GUN FIGHTER HAD A SPEED OF 300 M.P.H. ALTHOUGH OUTPACED BY THE GERMAN MESSERSCHMITT 109, IT WAS A POWERFUL WEAPON IN SKILLED HANDS.

"ACHTUNG — SPITFIRE!" THIS CRY ECHOED OVER THE INTERCOMS OF GERMAN PILOTS, HERALDING THE ARRIVAL OF THE GREATEST FIGHTER IN THE BATTLE.

SUPERIOR TO ANY ENEMY AIRCRAFT, IT WROUGHT HAVOC AMONG THE GERMANS.

THE FIGHTER PILOTS OF THE R.A.F. WORE THESE FAMOUS WINGS ON THEIR UNIFORM. MANY OF THEM, TOO, WORE THE MAUVE RIBBON OF THE D.F.C. — THE DISTINGUISHED FLYING CROSS — OR THE D.F.M. — THE DISTINGUISHED FLYING MEDAL — IN RECOGNITION OF THEIR GALLANTRY.

THE VALIANT THEME

★

THE VIKINGS, THE GREAT SAILOR-WARRIORS OF SCANDINAVIA, FIRST RAIDED BRITISH SHORES IN 795 A WHEN TH ROUNDED NORTHERN TIP OF SC IN FAMOUS LONG SHIPS AND LANDED IN IRELAND.

★

IN 865 A.D. THE VIKINGS INVADED ENGLAND, AND OCCUPIED THE KINGDOMS OF NORTHUMBRIA, MERCIA, AND EAST ANGLIA. LATER, THEY WERE DEFEATED BY KING ALFRED AT EDINGTON, AND THEIR LEADER, GUTHRUN, BECAME A CHRISTIAN.

THE MOST OUTSTANDING OF THE VIKINGS' FEATS WAS THE DISCOVERY OF AMERICA IN THE 10TH CENTURY A.D. A BAND OF VIKINGS UNDER LEIF ERICSSON SET OUT TO RAID MERCHANT SHIPS. BUT A FURIOUS STORM BLEW THEM WESTWARDS — AND THEY EVENTUALLY LANDED ON THE

War was the dominant theme of Fifties' and Sixties' comics. The Second World War dominated all war stories and these Valiant covers reflect the battle-hardened nature of the contents. Valiant's war stories made it Britain's top-selling boys' comic for several years, and no concessions were made to the enemy; Germans were "Krauts" and Italians were "Ities" thoughout the stories.

Early Seventies' comics Whizzer and Chips, and Cor!. together sold more than 900,000 copies of their first issue print run.

A FLOOD-TIDE OF "FUNNIES"

By channelling all their efforts into better "adventure" comic stories, and particularly by breaking new ground with publications like "Look and Learn" and the boys' magazine "Ranger", Fleetway kept their 50 per cent market share and learned a lesson that was to stand them in good stead - that in a volatile market a broad base of product is better than a couple of high-flying titles with nothing else to support them.

In the event, though, their decision to close down their humour titles, with the exception of the prosperous Buster, proved to be a premature one. For in 1970 a change of management reversed the decision and a flood of humour comics poured out of Fleetway House.

Whizzer and Chips ("Tremendous fun – two comics in one!"); Cor, Monster Fun, Krazy, all made money, each leaving the launch pad at a staggering 520,000 print run and generally ending their first week with sales around 460,000 to 470,000. Today, interestingly, a similar comic launch would print at around 150,000 and the publishers would be very content with a sale of 90,000.

Although comics have their ups and downs, and the market constantly shifts and changes, the general sales trend of any newly launched picture-strip comic in the U.K. is almost always irreversibly downwards, and that is as true today as when Dad was a boy.

You can ascribe it to fierce competition, or to the rapid turnover in readership, or to new non-publishing products vying for children's pocket money, or to insufficient publicity in the ongoing situation, or what you will, but whatever happens to the market total, the individual total too often has a predictable term to its life.

Of course, there have been and there still are notable exceptions to that trend. But as a general rule the publisher has two marketing choices: he can either spend his allotted budget reinforcing his existing titles and thereby eschewing new launches, or he can let his existing titles sink or swim and spend his money on new ones.

The first option makes hard work of life, because it attempts to buck the trend that even the news trade accepts (it may protest that it doesn't accept the trend, but it does). Additionally, there aren't many comics' publishers who can afford to spend the money which would be required to maintain any one title's presence in the market. The second option, at which Fleetway became the experts, creates its own myriad problems, but when Dad was a boy it worked.

Film Fun near the end of its life in 1956. This grand old comic ran for 20 years, and copies are now highly prized by collectors.

BIRTHPLACE OF THE TRIGAN EMPIRE

An unknown space ship crashes on Earth—and the strangest space story ever told begins.

The RISE and FALL of the TRIGAN EMPIRE

THROUGH the ice-cold vastness of outer space hurtled a cosmo craft – huge, unearthly, and out of control . . .

. . . out of control – as it had been for eight billion miles, see-sawing wildly,

. . . out of control for the most final of all reasons – THERE WAS A DEAD HAND ON THE ASTRO-HELM.

Indeed, the craft was manned by a crew that had been frozen to death.

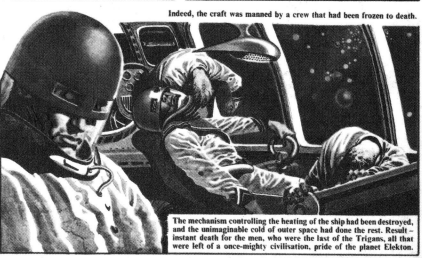

The mechanism controlling the heating of the ship had been destroyed, and the unimaginable cold of outer space had done the rest. Result – instant death for the men, who were the last of the Trigans, all that were left of a once-mighty civilisation, pride of the planet Elekton.

Then a mighty meteor plunged towards the spaceship, blazing furiously and howling like Gabriel's trumpet.

But the dead slept on and the meteor missed the cosmo craft close enough to alter its veering course and aim it – at EARTH!

This was the top boys' adventure story for a decade

RANGER
THE NATIONAL BOYS' MAGAZINE

EVERY MONDAY

FREE
INSIDE
A
GIFT
FOR
YOU

A
SUPERB
BOOKLET
THE
BOAC
VC10
WONDER
AIRCRAFT
OF THE AGE

Ranger, launched in 1965, attempted to become a genuine boys' magazine with a good deal of feature material supported by picture strip stories. One of its stories was "The Trigan Empire", a tale of life in Outer Space that was the favourite boys' story for ten years. Ranger lasted only nine months. On its death "The Trigan Empire" was transferred into Look and Learn. The magazine failed against comics' opposition which included the popular Lion; boys of Dad's generation quickly showed that they didn't want a magazine at nearly three times the price of a comic.

RANGER:
Bobby Moore, Macbeth and a bit of Biggles

BOBBY MOORE'S

WORLD OF SPORT

Bobby Moore, captain of England and West Ham, writes for RANGER every week.

This week: PIPPED ON THE POST!

Yorkshireman Tommy Simpson, one of the world's greatest cyclists, is never likely to forget his last-second victory in this year's 280 mile race from London to Holyhead. After hours of pedalling on the roads through England and into Wales the 38 crack cyclists approached Holyhead. Three men flashed to the finishing line almost shoulder to shoulder—and Tommy Simpson was first to cross it, only a tyre's width in front of his nearest rival. What a finish after 280 miles of non-stop racing at a record average of 25.7 miles an hour!

▶ Brian Phelps was only 13 when he was first chosen to represent Britain in an international diving contest. That was in 1957. A year later this perky East Ham schoolboy, who took up high diving when he was just a tiny 9-year-old, became the youngest and the smallest member of Britain's team for the European Championships at Budapest. It was a great honour for young Brian but no one expected him to win any medals. But Brian, standing less than 5 feet tall, feared no one. His diving was sensational. The Russians were brilliant, too, but after a final dive that sent the crowd wild with delight, the East London schoolboy won the gold medal.

◀ Belle Vue, Manchester, was packed with jubilant fight fans on November 30, 1964. Terry Downes, the tearaway terror from London, was meeting Willie Pastrano, the hard-hitting American, in a fight for the world light - heavyweight championship. Pastrano was the champion and cheery Terry wanted that title. From the first bell the fight was a sizzler and the confident Cockney slammed the champion all round the ring. As round followed round the fans roared louder—for Terry Downes seemed as if he was on the way to the greatest victory

England were playing Scotland in a Rugby international at Twickenham in March this year. In the second half the Scots took a lead of three points (for a dropped goal) and looked like winning their first game at Twickenham for 27 years. Then, with only seconds to go, Andy Hancock, England's left-wing, started one of the most fantastic runs ever seen at Twickenham. Beating man after man he sprinted nearly 90 yards before scoring a brilliant try. England had robbed Scotland of victory in the last few seconds!

▼

Ranger's mix was all things to all boys. Bobby Moore was captain of England's 1966 World Cup winning team. Most boys had some idea who Macbeth was, but they didn't rate him in this form.

continue—but the referee stepped between the two boxers and awarded the

Shakespeare's powerful story of the man who blazed a trail of bloodshed to Scotland's Throne — presented as it has never been told before

The ADVENTURES of MACBETH

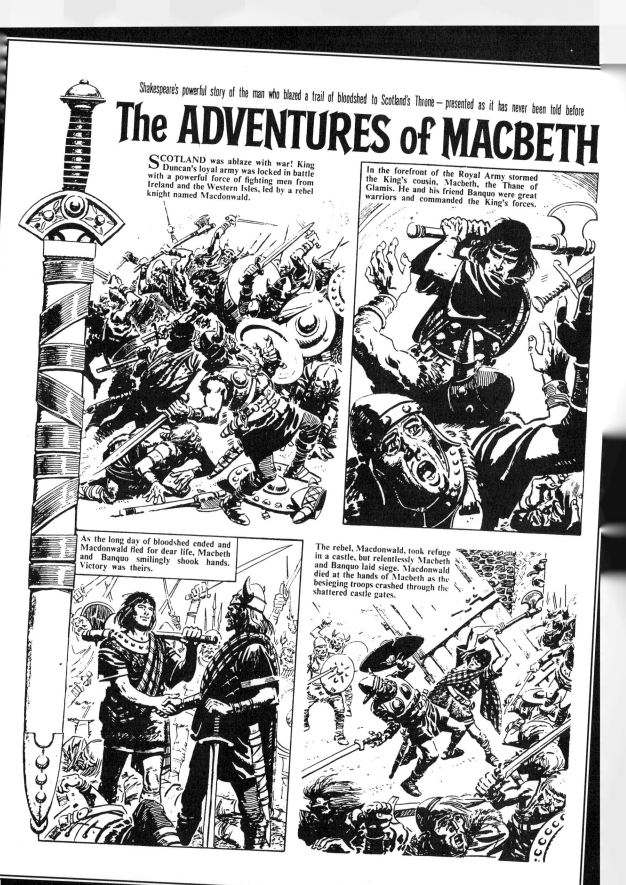

SCOTLAND was ablaze with war! King Duncan's loyal army was locked in battle with a powerful force of fighting men from Ireland and the Western Isles, led by a rebel knight named Macdonwald.

In the forefront of the Royal Army stormed the King's cousin, Macbeth, the Thane of Glamis. He and his friend Banquo were great warriors and commanded the King's forces.

As the long day of bloodshed ended and Macdonwald fled for dear life, Macbeth and Banquo smilingly shook hands. Victory was theirs.

The rebel, Macdonwald, took refuge in a castle, but relentlessly Macbeth and Banquo laid siege. Macdonwald died at the hands of Macbeth as the besieging troops crashed through the shattered castle gates.

COMEDY CAPERS
at 3d a week

Knockout, launched in 1939 by the Amalgamated Press, was still going when Dad was a boy. Its front-page heros, Deed-a-Day Danny and Stonehenge Kit, the Ancient Brit, were in the tradition of D.C. Thomson's Beano and Dandy. Its back page Sporty strip shown here was drawn by Reg Woolton, creator of the Sporting Sam cartoon in the Sunday Express. Knockout died in the Fifties but the title was successfully revived in the Seventies and lasted another five years.

HATCH, MATCH AND DESPATCH

...that was the formula behind successful comics' publishing

Dad can probably recall even to this day the bewildering plethora of new comics that rained on to his newsagent's counter as he grew into his teens. Some lasted only months, some lasted decades. Describing that period of frenetic publishing activity when Dad was a lad, a distinguished history of comics declared:

"Market research is extensively employed to safeguard the capital outlay in launching a new comic."

Nothing could be farther from the truth. Comics' publishers rarely used market research – there was never time enough for it. Gut feel was all that mattered. And when gut feel was wrong and a new launch became a failure, Dad will remember the publishers' trick of "merging" it with another title.

Merging a failing title into a prosperous one worked because at least in the first week of the merge the news trade would generally sell up to 90 per cent of the combined sales figure of

the two titles before they were merged. So if a successful title were selling 100,000 copies, and it became host to an unsuccessful one selling 50,000 copies, sales for the joint title would be 90 per cent of 150,000, or 135,000.

Accept that the smaller title was losing money anyway, and you can see that the successful title suddenly received a 35 per cent increase in sales for which it had paid nothing. Add to this the cost reductions obtained by producing one publication instead of two, and you were on the way to doubling the profits

A year or two after discovering how well this formula worked, comics' publishers were seriously considering launching "controlled failures" just as "merger material" for their successful titles! Fortunately, they never actually did so; the interests of the readers, and the staff who would have to work on "controlled failures", were put above such tawdry commercial considerations.

> **He that hides treasure**
> **Imagines every one thinks of**
> **that place.**
>
> THOMAS MIDDLETON.

The illustrations and the quotation on this page are all from Sixties boys' publications

LOOK! THE DEVIL YOU SEEK HAS SOUGHT *YOU!*

After the merge, what happened next? Well, the pattern was predicatable. The joint title would start to lose the sales that had been added to it over a period of some months. Sometimes it might take a year to return to its pre-merge figure. The profits accruing for the publisher over these weeks were, of course, impressive. Although the idea of "controlled failures" was never taken up, "hatch, match and despatch" thus became a favourite philosophy.

But at the sharp end, where Dad was, the reader began to wonder how many more defunct comics' names could possibly be crammed on to the title page of his current favourite comic. Example of one that actually happened: Whizzer and Chips and Monster Fun and Krazy. At one stage when the four extant Disney comics were having circulation problems, the publishers seriously considered merging them all, to have one title which could have been called "Mickey Mouse and Donald Duck with Pluto incorporating Goofy."

TIGER

Incorporating THE CHAMPION

The SPORT and ADVENTURE PICTURE STORY WEEKLY

3D

EVERY TUESDAY

No. 29. March 26, 1955

Roy of the ROVERS

By Stewart Colwyn

ROY RACE, CENTRE-FORWARD OF MELCHESTER ROVERS RESERVES, HAD RECEIVED LETTERS THREATENING TROUBLE FOR THE TEAM IF HE DIDN'T OBEY MYSTERIOUS ORDERS. NOT KNOWING WHAT THE ORDERS WERE, ROY COULD DO NOTHING. THEN, JUST BEFORE A MATCH AGAINST WELBECK WANDERERS, HALF THE TEAM FOUND THEIR BOOTS MISSING, AND HAD TO PLAY IN BORROWED, MAKESHIFT BOOTS... ROY WAS FORCED TO WEAR HIS ORDINARY SHOES!

ROY SLIPPED HEADLONG AS HE TRIED TO BEAT THE WELBECK CENTRE-HALF, BUT HE QUICKLY SCRAMBLED TO HIS FEET AND LEAPT FORWARD.

I'LL SHOOT FIRST TIME! —OH, DARN THESE SHOES! I'VE SLICED IT!

THE FANS GROANED AS THE BALL SPUN WILDLY OUT TO THE WING.

WHAT IN THUNDER IS RACE PLAYING AT?

DO YOU WONDER HE'S SLIDING ALL OVER THE PLACE? FANCY PLAYING IN ORDINARY SHOES!

MANAGER BEN GALLOWAY, SITTING WITH THE DIRECTORS, SEETHED WITH ANGER.

RACE PLAYED BADLY ENOUGH IN THE FIRST HALF! NOW HE CAN'T EVEN GET NEAR THE GOAL! I SHALL DEMAND AN EXPLANATION OF ALL THIS!

EXACTLY, GALLOWAY! THE BOARD OF DIRECTORS WILL WANT TO KNOW WHO'S RESPONSIBLE FOR THE MISSING BOOTS, AND WHY RACE IS PLAYING IN HIS SHOES!

BUT NEXT MOMENT, BEN FORGOT HIS ANNOYANCE. THE ROVERS RIGHT WINGER BEAT A BACK TO THE BALL, AND SWUNG OVER A HIGH CENTRE.

WE'RE TWO DOWN! I MUSTN'T MISS THIS TIME! I CAN'T TRUST MY FEET—BUT I CAN USE MY HEAD!

ROY MADE A SPECTACULAR LEAP, AND....

GOAL! GOAL!

GOOD OLD ROY! THAT'S MORE LIKE IT!

PLEASE TURN TO BACK PAGE.

Roy of the Rovers first ran on to the pitch at Melchester in Tiger in 1954, when his manager, Ben Galloway, wore a bowler hat. In the 1970s he was tranferred into a new comic that bore his name and is still published today. Roy's superb goal-scoring skills made him a journalists' and sports commentators' cliche: "It was real Roy of the Rovers stuff" is a phrase that has entered the English language.

"SKY-HIGH" TALES

IT REALLY STARTED THE DAY OF THE SPEED TEST — THAT FATEFUL MORNING WHEN THE NEW LANKESTER "LIGHTNING" MOTOR TORPEDO-BOAT WAS PUT THROUGH HER PACES BEFORE A SMALL PRIVILEGED CROWD ON THE WHARF OF LANKESTER'S BOATYARD

Some men go out to seek danger. Others don't have to look for it. It just comes to them! And Matt Crosby was one of the latter kind...

THOUGH MATT CROSBY WAS ONLY A HUMBLE MECHANIC IN THE LANKESTER YARD, HE THRILLED WITH PRIDE AS HE OVERHEARD ONE OF THE "TOP BRASS" NAVAL MEN SPEAK TO LAURENCE LANKESTER

IT'S A WONDER CRAFT, LANKESTER! AMAZING ACCELERATION! WHAT SPEED DO YOU HOPE TO ACHIEVE?

BUT EVEN AS THE TEST PILOT WAS OPENING THE THROTTLE, HE WAS HORRIFIED TO SEE A HUGE BAULK OF TIMBER FLOATING HALF-SUBMERGED DEAD AHEAD!

LOOK OUT, SIR!

HE SWUNG THE HELM HARD OVER, SENDING THE SPEEDING CRAFT SLEWING VIOLENTLY TO PORT — ONLY TO SEE ANOTHER BAULK OF TIMBER IN HIS PATH!

All Dad's heros were square-jawed and clean-cut. Here Lion's "Sky-High" Bannion bears a remarkable resemblance to Eagle's super-hero, Dan Dare.

When Dad was a boy there were broadly speaking two distinct categories of comics. There were "humour" comics, intended to make his sides ache with laughter, or "adventure" comics, intended to make his eyes pop with excitement.

Very occasionally, a "humour" comic like Buster gave over its centre spread to an adventure story. Much more frequently, an "adventure" comic carried a funny page. But in both cases these "extras" were there only to change the pace, and Dad and his pals expected "funnies" to be in a "humour" comic, and excitement to be in an "adventure" comic.

Way out in front in the circulation race for "humour" comics were the D.C. Thomson pair Beano and Dandy. Like all "humour" comics they were, and still are, unisex, although probably read more by boys than by girls. Dad might have been one of the million and a half kids who bought one or other or both of them – and his Dad might have been, too!

Beano and Dandy were the Thomson flagships, and Thomson dominated the "humour" market. The reason for that was almost all a matter of economics. "Humour" comics traditionally had lower cover prices than "adventure" comics, and since the comics' publisher enjoys little or no advertisement revenue, and his income is therefore only from circulation sales, that meant he had to sell more "humour" comics than "adventure" comics to cover costs.

As circulation sales dipped, D.C. Thomson, riding on very high sales, could afford to take a knock or two. Their rivals in the south, the Amalgamated Press, who didn't sell as many, felt the draught more acutely. They had such tried and tested "humour" titles as Radio Fun and Film Fun, based on existing entertainers, and in the "own-brand" sector they had Knockout. But they weren't winning the price war, and any impartial observer could see that Thomson had incontestably the better publications.

ROCKFIST ROGAN – FIGHTER PILOT of WORLD WAR II

By HAL WILTON

In 1940, England stood alone while hordes of Nazi aircraft were hurled against her. Only the Spitfires and Hurricanes of the Royal Air Force shielded her from these vicious attacks Among the pilots of these planes, none was more fearless and daring than Rockfist Rogan . . .

FIGHTING "ROUND THE CLOCK"!

WAAARRRRH!
Rockfist Rogan dived his bullet-riddled fighter out of the war-torn skies of Kent. Behind him swept his two pals, Curly Hooper and Archie Streatham.
Together the three planes roared towards the airfield which was their base—one of the front line fighter stations in the Battle of Britain.
Rockfist and his pals were members of

previous day.
"He was seen baling out over the French coast. I don't think he came to any harm," Rockfist said.
"I was darned sorry he lost that pla though. This replacement th me has been patched so hardly any of the original job
The flight to which Whac had been doing a turn of Rockfist and his pals were brief rest, and because of t

"You'll have to drink it yourself." Rockfist shouted.
Rockfist was about to boost himself into the cockpit when he uttered an exclamation of disgust and looked at a cky mess on his hands.
"Dyall," he yelled furiously. "How any more times do I have to tell you? hen you do one of your painting jobs n my kite don't park your chewing gum the cockpit!"
"So that's where I left it!" said Dizzy ightly.
"Grrrr!" growled Rockfist as he ropped into the plane.
There were times when he felt Dizzy o be a bigger menace than the Nazis.
Rockfist plugged in his earphones to btain directions from the radio control-oom. Seconds later he sent his plane creaming into the air. Curly and Archie ame roaring up behind him.
Suddenly Rockfist let out an excited yell.
"Tally-ho!"
He had spotted the enemy raiders—

Tiger continued to publish text stories in 1955, but Dad's generation didn't want them. Perhaps one of the things they didn't like was that this Rockfist Rogan story was first published in Champion fifteen years earlier!

I f D.C. Thomson in Dundee were well ahead of the field in the "humour" comics" market when Dad was a boy, and they were providing most of the laughs through such brilliantly original characters as Desperate Dan and Lord Snooty and his Pals, Fleetway had the edge on them when it came to pure thrills and adventure.

The two companies had 95 per cent of the market between them, and the formula for the boys' "adventure" comics they produced was identical. The publications were 32 pages, they were printed in letterpress – an extremely cheap printing method – their cover prices were as low as possible, and if you were lucky there might be four pages of ghastly colour (front, back, and centre spread) in what was otherwise a sea of muddy grey.

They were marketed for what they were

intended to be, very cheap and highly disposable. But the story contents followed a close formula, and the many and varied writers who had failed in the adult markets and imagined that they could cover themselves with glory in what looked to be "simple" picture-strip stories, soon discovered that this was a much harder nut to crack than many adult markets.

Thus it was, too, with the art. Both companies bought their art work from all over the world and they paid well for it, although Fleetway's rates were generally much higher than their Scottish rivals.

Eschewing the "humour" market, the London-based company produced a clutch of "adventure" comics that were to prove a deep thorn in the side of Thomson's Hotspur, Wizard, and Adventure, all of which were getting past their zenith.

THE OLD AND THE NEW IN 'FUNNIES'

Only half a dozen mid-century years separated these two comics. Comic Cuts launched in 1890 lasted 63 years, and Buster, launched in 1958, is still being published today as a monthly. The contrasting styles reflect Comic Cuts as a sixty-year-old, and Buster as a three-year-old.

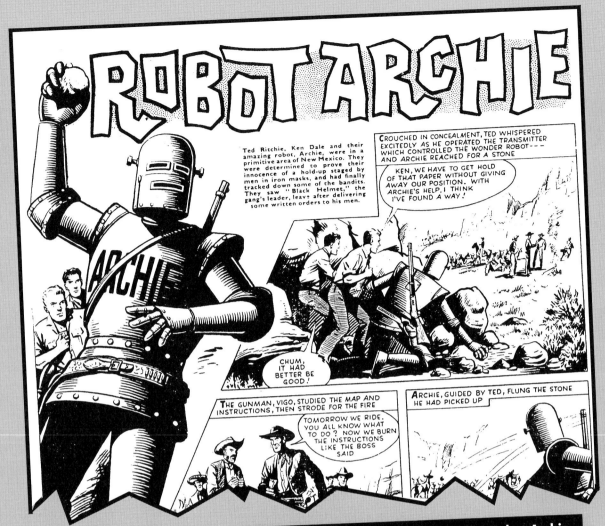

Top of the pops with Lion readers was Robot Archie, a cybernetic superman long before any of the robotic TV and film favourites of later years.

HOW LION AND VALIANT
put the excitement into Sixties' schooldays

First among the Fleetway newcomers was Lion; then came Hurricane, Tiger and Valiant. The Thomson response to this onslaught was Victor, a comic which showed all the clever touches of the Thomson editors but which couldn't meet the cavalry charge on its own.

Arguably the most successful of Fleetway's highly successful launches at this time was Tiger, if only for the fact that it boasted the new and immediately popular soccer hero Roy Race, who played for Melchester Rovers. Roy of the Rovers is how Dad remembers him in his own comic today. Roy is still being published every week in his own comic.

In fact, it wasn't until a quarter of a century later, when Tiger was still going strong and attracting first name pieces by stars like Geoff Boycott and Gary Lineker, that Roy was extrapolated from Tiger and launched in the comic named after him.

Today, Tiger is dead. Roy of the Rovers magazine is now a cross between a comic and a soccer magazine, and its hero, who plays across four pages every week, must be in his sixties if he began playing with Melchester in Tiger while still a teenager. Still, that sort of judgment on comic heros has to be suspended, for Mickey Mouse was born in 1928 and Billy Bunter, who you can still see around occasionally, is getting on for eighty!

Just as Buster was never the equal of Beano or Dandy, so Victor never hit the story quality of Lion or Valiant. As for the stories themselves, the one subject that was way out in front of all the others was heroics in the Second World War.

Social analysts have gone over and over again this phenomenon of comics in Dad's day – why it was, twenty years after the war had ended, that the favourite theme was always the war. Some argue that it was because post-war Britain was in a state of constant decline, and the war represented the apogee of Britain's fame in the eyes of the rest of the world. It mattered not at all that the rest of the world had long since forgotten 1940 and all that; we are an insular race and can easily wrap ourselves up in ourselves.

Others put it all down to a mix of British jingosim and xenophobia. But there was probably more truth in the editors' simplistic view that boys' stories have to be about heroics, and the Second World War just happened to be the most recent thing in heroics.

Certainly this view was backed up with the fact that boys of Dad's generation hadn't the slightest interest in space stories. The real thing, in the shape of the Apollo project and the Sputniks, was going on all around them in the media. But a broad sweep through comic readers of Dad's generation at that time showed that they were generally unimpressed with outer space conquest; they seemed to find it clinical, technical and boring.

What was wrong with the space race as story material perhaps was the fact that it wasn't the men who were doing the achieving so much as the machines, and machines are not the stuff of a good story. So it had to be the Second World War, and when German comics' publishers, who occasionally bought British stories, expressed their astonishment at this "unhealthy" trend, the British rejoinder echoed Mandy Rice-Davis's famous Court-room aphorism, "Well, they would, wouldn't they?"

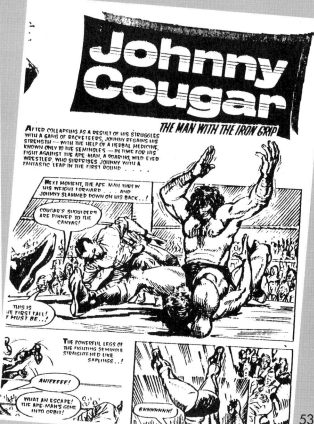

HOW TV BEGAN TO DOMINATE THE WORLD OF COMICS

Virgil and Brains are in the Mole following the tracks of a giant machine which a gang of crooks are using to cause earthquakes. Suddenly the Mole bores through an undersea cliff . . .

54

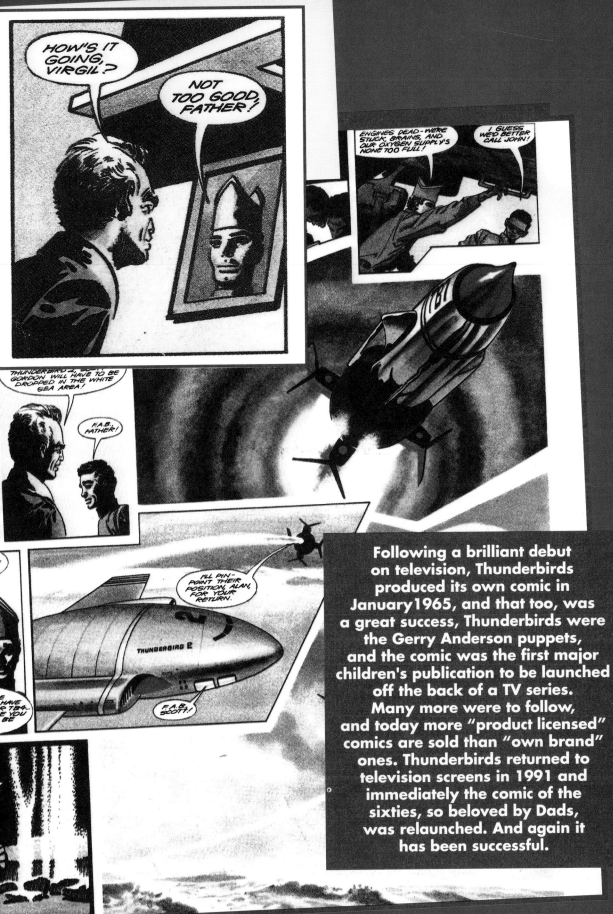

Following a brilliant debut on television, Thunderbirds produced its own comic in January 1965, and that too, was a great success, Thunderbirds were the Gerry Anderson puppets, and the comic was the first major children's publication to be launched off the back of a TV series. Many more were to follow, and today more "product licensed" comics are sold than "own brand" ones. Thunderbirds returned to television screens in 1991 and immediately the comic of the sixties, so beloved by Dads, was relaunched. And again it has been successful.

TO GLORY WE

His Majesty's frigate 'Lowestoffe' had just been fired on by an American privateer. On board was the young Lieutenant Horatio Nelson...

★

Captain Locker brought his ship round in a scudding turn, and 'Lowestoffe' heeled over sharply as the gale strained against her canvas . . .

SHE SPOKE WITH THE THUNDEROUS CANNONADE OF A FULL BROADSIDE ~~ A DEAFENING THUNDERCLAP OF ORANGE FLAME AND RED-HOT SHOT.

THE BO'SUN'S PIPE SHRILLED ABOARD THE 'LOWESTOFFE' AS STRUGGLING SEAMEN STRAINED TO LOWER THE LONGBOAT INTO THE WATER ~~

I CALL FOR VOLUNTEERS TO GO ABOARD THE PRIVATEER AND CLAIM HER AS A PRIZE ~~ AND I'M WARNING YOU, LADS, THAT IN THIS SEA, 'TWILL BE A HAZARDOUS TASK!

I WILL CONSIDER IT AN HONOUR TO COMMAND THE LONGBOAT, SIR!

FOLLOWING YOUNG LIEUTENANT NELSON'S EXAMPLE, THERE WAS NO SHORTAGE OF VOLUNTEERS TO MAN THE LONGBOAT ~~ AND SOON THE FRAIL CRAFT WAS AFLOAT IN THAT GALE-TORN SEA ~~ AND HEADING FOR THE DISMASTED PRIVATEER ~~

AYE! AND IF LIEUTENANT NELSON IS TO BE WITH US, YOU CAN COUNT ON ME, SIR!

AFTER AN HOUR OF BACK-BREAKING TOIL, DURING WHICH TIME THE ANGRY WAVES THREATENED TO SWAMP THEM A SCORE OF TIMES, NELSON BROUGHT HIS BOAT ALONGSIDE THE WALLOWING PRIVATEER ~~

AHOY THERE! I ORDER YOU TO THROW US A LINE!

THE AMERICANS OBEYED. A LINE WAS THROWN ~~ AND SOON NELSON WAS TREADING THE HEELING DECKS OF HIS FIRST PRIZE-SHIP.

CAPTAIN NAT PARKER OF THE PRIVATEER, BOSTON LADY, AT YOUR SERVICE, SIR!

THE AMERICAN CAPTAIN'S [...] TWINKLED WITH AMUSEMENT [...] SWORD TO THE COOL [...]

BILLY BRAVE and the GAMES MASTER'S SECRET

[...] ARE RACING TOWARDS TOR MANOR [A]BOUT A BOX OF SILVER PLATE, WHICH [...]NS HAVE JUST STOLEN FROM THEM....

COME ON, ERIC. LET'S BEARD THE OLD LION IN HIS DEN!

REALLY, YOU BOYS ~~~

QUICK! CAN WE SEE MR RIVERS ~~ IT'S TERRIBLY IMPORTANT

BILLY AND ERIC FACE THE IRATE OWNER OF TOR MANOR AND TELL THEIR STORY

THIS IS A MOST EXTRAORDINARY STORY. I WILL PHONE THE POLICE AT ONCE

THE SILVER PLATE WAS STOLEN FROM HERE SOME TIME AGO, BUT THE PERSON WHO DID IT ~~~

THOSE TOUGHS DID IT, SIR

MY BOY, YOU MAY HAVE HELPED TO RIGHT A TERRIBLE WRONG. WILL YOU TAKE A MESSAGE BACK TO YOUR GAMES MASTER FOR ME!

LATER, ON THE WAY BACK TO MANNINGTON

I WONDER WHAT'S WRITTEN IN THIS NOTE FOR WADDON?

Eric Parker drew a number of military and naval stories for Dad's comics, like 'To Glory we Steer' for Lion. 'Billy Brave' was published in Mickey Mouse in 1957.

STANDING IN THE STERN SHEETS, CLOSE TO THE TILLER, STOOD THE FEARLESS NELSON.

Dad and his pals loved Second World War stories. While he was swotting for his O levels, he relaxed, for example with Paddy Payne, Warrior of the Skies, on Lion's front page. Payne was the R.A.F's trouble-shooter, a sort of latter-day Rockfist Rogan, and there was no trouble made that he couldn't shoot. Towards the back of the comic Dad could also read Captain Condor and the War in Space, but Condor was never as popular as Payne; given a choice between a Spitfire and a space rocket, the Spitfire won every time.

How was all this known, in the almost complete absence of market research? Three or four times a year, when Dad was reading the readers' letters column, he may have noticed a form to cut out and send in with any letter he cared to write to the Editor.

The form asked him to name his favourite three stories and his three "least liked" stories. Since there were usually only seven stories in the comic, and since boys will always dutifully oblige with this kind of information, Editors had a pretty good up-to-date view of what their readers wanted.

What always rated in the first three on the questionnaire was the off-beat story – something Lion was particularly good at. One of the best off-beat stories was Robot Archie, a steel-clad figure that thought and fought like a human. Because he was all made of metal, Archie had that intriguing attraction that some comic characters are gifted with – you never saw his eyes. In future years artists and editors were to recognise the mystery that surrounds the eyeless: Andy Capp and Judge Dredd are two other favourites whose eyes you can never look into.

FIZZY ROCKET
Science fiction might not have worked in Dad's day, but that didn't stop publishers having a go at it. So a new comics' publisher, the News of the World, produced Rocket in 1956, calling it the first space age weekly.

Rocket was a 16-page tabloid with Battle of Britain hero Douglas Bader in the Editor's chair. Sadly for Bader, Rocket didn't get into orbit, fizzing out in the year of its launch. Dad was grown up when, twenty years later, a sci-fi comic was launched with a super-hero who has already passed into the comics' hall of fame – 2000 AD, with its incredible Judge Dredd.

When Dad was a tiny tot, publishers fought for his pennies

Nº1 *OF A GRAND NEW PAPER FOR BOYS AND GIRLS*

PLAYHOUR PICTURES

No. 1
October 16, 1964

4p

PRINCE – The wonder dog of the golden west

Here is Prince the wonder dog, pride of the rolling prairies, with his master Texas Jack, the famous Wild West scout. Beside Texas Jack stands Duke, the scout's great horse and loyal friend.

Prince was a puppy when Texas Jack took him from some ba men who were ill-treating him. The scout bound up the dog wounds and Prince has often repaid his master for saving his li

TINY TOTS 3ᴰ
ONCE A WEEK

No. 1,002
OUT ON
THURSDAY

The Little Ones' Own Paper

Tiny Tots

and THE SUNBEAM

3ᴰ

September 13ᵗʰ 1952

TI-NY AND TOT GO TO THE ZOO WITH NUR-SIE

1. Nur-sie has tak-en Ti-ny and Tot to a sea-side Zoo and they are look-ing for-ward to see-ing all the an-i-mals. "I want a ride on a cam-el," says Tot.

2. Tot en-joys her cam-el ride ver-y much, but Ti-ny wants his tea be-cause he is hun-gry. "I am a-fraid I have not e-nough mon-ey for tea!" sighs nur-sie.

3. All at once the child-ren see some pen-guins which have es-caped from their cage. "I know how to catch them," says Ti-ny, as he gets a lad-der.

4. Ti-ny holds one end of the lad-der and Tot, the oth-er, then they run a-long to the pen-guins. "Now low-er the lad-der o-ver their heads!" says Ti-ny.

5. Now the pen-guins are pris-on-ers, and Ti-ny and Tot lead them

6. And such a nice

'Nursery' comics, as these publications were called, were targeted at the under-sevens, and they formed a thriving market in the Fifties', Sixties' and Seventies'. Old established titles like Tiny Tots split each syllable in each word with a hyphen, to facilitate reading. Playhour, launched in 1954, soon abandoned its editorial slant of trying to be a junior version of a boys' adventure comic with its Wild West cover story, and began to run stories that were more suitable for little children. The circulation then leapt. In the early 1970s Playhour sold 330,000 copies a week – ten times more than any one of the few nursery publications left sells today.

GOAL! How football became the boys' own winner.

The age of the "specialist" comic was still a long way off. Dad's comics in the "adventure" genre were always a mix of stories – a war story, an off-beat story, occasionally a sci-fi story, a sports story, and so on. Sport, the one area where you would have thought Dad's generation would have accepted a specialist comic, attracted no takers.

Things were beginning to change, though. A company specialising in trade journals brought out a football magazine called Goal in the 1960s, and, although no one said so for fear of scaring off advertisers, Goal was almost exclusively read by boys.

The new soccer magazine was weekly, and therefore up-to-date, expensive, but good to be seen around with if you were a juvenile soccer fan, and it rapidly developed a successful style of sports writing that was appropriate for its young market – a style that has since been picked up by other soccer magazines beamed at the young market.

Goal knew what the boys wanted: big colour action pictures, hero-worshipping biographies, and encapsulated information about soccer's big stars – the new super-heroes. But the magazine didn't keep its eye on the ball. It was swamped in 1970 by the much more energetic Shoot!, launched by Fleetway, who snapped up the rival publication for £7,000 and merged it into their new publication.

The launch of Shoot! was attendant on one of the very rare market research exercises undertaken in the comic market. The pivotal question was whether boys wanted a mix of fact and fiction in one title. The

Tiny Tots was one of several "Nursery" comics that flourished between the two World Wars and lasted into the Fifties. Like all these older comics, it refused to abandon even towards the end of its days a curious habit of breaking up the syllables of polysyllabic words. The idea was that it helped young children to read. Mod-ern teach-ers pro-bab-ly would-n't acc-ept that i-dea. "Nursery" comics launched in the Fifties and Sixties chose a much simpler approach (The Simple Simon strip was published in Playhour), with big pictures, short captions and no split words.

answer was unequivocably negative.

Those who wanted fiction only and those who wanted fact only were in polarised camps, fifty per cent in each. Thus Shoot! was launched as a "fact" publication on the Goal formula – all news, photographs and topical features.. What the market research could claim, of course, was that the launch of Shoot! left the other 50 per cent of young soccer fans unsatisified.

So, a couple of years later, Scorcher, all football fiction, was launched from the same camp. It worked well for five years, then it was merged into Tiger. A good few years have gone by since Dad was a comic reader. As with all other industries in our era of change, a good few things have happened to comics, too.

Most significant is that fewer boys read them (many people hold that fewer boys actually read), and the comics they do read are much more specialised – they reflect a particular television programme or entertainment segment, like football or science fiction.

Ten years ago other Dads dealt comics a reeling blow from which they are now at last beginning slowly to recover. This was the computer revolution, in which Dads were hyped into believing that if their sons became "computer literate" they would probably earn £50,000 a year by the time they were 21.

It was all so much nonsense, of course, particularly when the vast majority of these young computer buffs never progressed beyond the games-playing stage. But by then £400 of the family budget had been spent on the hardwear and softwear, and reading had been relegated to second place in favour of zapping.

Happily, there are signs of a slow recovery in comic sales. Computer games are finding their proper insignificant level and the joy of reading is being rediscovered. Comics won't be the same, but having weathered the storm, they will always be here.

How will they look? Will there be new frontiers to be crossed, new market gaps to be explored? For the answers, you'll need to read the Dad's Own Annual that your son will buy for your grandson in about 25 years time!

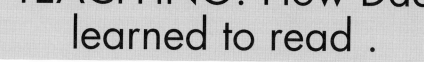

TEACH-ING! How Dad learned to read .

A Tuck-me-up Tale For The Lit-tle Ones!

TEACH-ING SPOT A LES-SON

MA-VIS and Maur-ice were twins, had just had a birth-day. They five can-dles on their cake, show-ed they were five years old. Mu had giv-en Ma-vis a sweet lit-tle grey ki and dad-dy had giv-en Maur-ice a sauc-y fat podge of pup-py.

Ma-vis named her kit-ten Smo-ky

one eye which made him look ver
Now Spot had been a ver-y na
Do you know what he had done
stol-en poor Smo-ky's din-ner, and e
his own, as well! The twins gave
scold-ing, but he did not look a b
Poor Smo-ky cried for her din-n
child-ren had to ask mum-my to
more food for the kit-ten.

- TINY TOTS -

UNCLE JACK'S JOLLY PAGE

SHARP EYES ?

TINY TOTS Office,
The Fleetway House,
Farringdon Street,
London, E.C.4.

Dear Lit-tle Friend,—Lit-tle girls are fond of writ-ing se-cret let-ters on the backs of their en-vel-opes. Years a-go, I was puz-zled when I first saw "SWALK" on the back of one. It took me a long time to guess that it meant "Sealed With A Loving Kiss"! Now a new one has pop-ped up. It is "TTFN." Would you be-lieve it? It means "Ta-ta For Now"!

POST CARD

To . . .
My Lit-tle Frie
Who-ev-er You A
Wher-ev-er Yo
In Great Brit-ai
Or O-ver the

UN-CLE JACK

RID-DLE

Why is a bad
like a post-age sta
Be-cause you li
and put him i